A place in space: the Moon

Written by Gill Munton

Speed Sounds

Consonants   *Ask children to say the sounds.*

f	l	m	n	r	s	v	z	sh	th	ng
ff	ll	mm	nn	rr	ss	ve	zz			**(nk)**
ph	le	mb	kn	wr	se		se			
					c		s			
					ce					

b	c	d	g	h	j	p	qu	t	w	x	y	ch
bb	k	dd	gg		g	pp		tt	wh			**(tch)**
	ck				ge							

Each box contains one sound but sometimes more than one grapheme.
*Focus graphemes for this story are **circled**.*

Vowels

Ask children to say the sounds in and out of order.

a	e	i	o	u	ay	ee	igh	ow
	ea				a-e	ea	i-e	o-e
						y	ie	o
						e	i	
at	hen	in	on	up	day	see	high	blow

oo	oo	ar	or	air	ir	ou	oy
u-e			oor	are	ur		oi
ue			ore		er		
			aw				
zoo	look	car	for	fair	whirl	shout	boy

Story Green Words

Ask children to read the words first in Fred Talk and then say the word.

Moon plane shape dark huge speed tanks
north south poles brave date fact Earth*

Ask children to say the syllables and then read the whole word.

A mer i can   Arm strong   Al d rin   A poll o 11
re flec ted   di a me ter   mod ule   De cem ber   lu nar*
hu mans*   as tro naut*

Ask children to read the root first and then the whole word with the suffix.

crater → craters   object → objects   hit → hitting
orbit → orbits   shine → shines   tide → tides
form → formed   land → landed   patch → patches

*Challenge Words

6

Vocabulary Check

Discuss the meaning (as used in the non-fiction text) after the children have read the word.

	definition
craters	holes
formed	made
orbits	goes round
reflected light	light shining back, like light from a mirror
tides	ebb and flow of the sea to and from land
diameter	distance across a ball shape
north, south	different directions
poles	top and bottom
lunar module	the small part of a spacecraft in which astronauts can land

Red Words

Ask children to practise reading the words across the rows, down the columns and in and out of order clearly and quickly.

any	do	does	other
there	they	was	water
were	what	who	to
of	ball	want	could
their	one	once	said

What does the Moon look like?

Up in space, far higher than any plane can go, is the Moon.

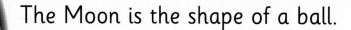

The Moon is the shape of a ball.

It has light patches — big hills — and dark patches — huge craters.

The craters were formed by space objects hitting the Moon at high speed.

What does the Moon do?

- The Moon orbits the Earth every 27.3 days.

  The same side always faces us, so we do not see the far side.

Moon

Earth

- It shines with reflected light from the Sun.

- It makes tides in the Earth's seas.

Moon fact

The Moon's diameter is about 3475 kilometres.

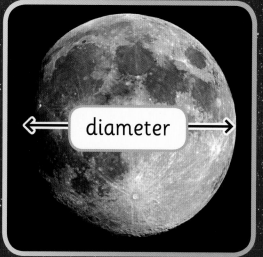

diameter

Is there life on the Moon?

air tank

There is no air on the Moon and there is no life. Astronauts who visit the Moon must take air with them in tanks.

an astronaut on the Moon

Moon fact

The Moon is about 384,400 kilometres from Earth.

There is no air, but there is water – ice has been found at the north and south poles.

north pole

south pole

Who has landed on the Moon?

Brave astronauts have made visits to the Moon six times.

No other place in space has been landed on by humans.

In 1969, American astronauts named Armstrong and Aldrin became the first humans to set foot on the Moon.

They landed in the lunar module of Apollo 11.

The date of the last Moon landing was December 1972.

Apollo 17

Who will be the next human to land on the Moon?

Questions to talk about

Ask children to TTYP for each question using 'Fastest finger' (FF) or 'Have a think' (HaT).

p.9 (FF) What are the dark patches on the Moon?

p.10 (FF) What makes the Moon shine?

p.11 (FF) What is the Moon's diameter?

p.12 (FF) Why do astronauts need air tanks?

p.13 (HaT) Where has ice been found on the Moon?

p.14 (FF) How many visits have been made to the Moon?

p.15 (HaT) Why do you think astronauts haven't been to the Moon recently?

Questions to read and answer

(Children complete without your help.)

1. What shape is the Moon?

2. What makes the tides in the sea?

3. What sort of water is on the Moon?

4. Who were the first men on the Moon?

5. When was the last Moon landing?